Edwin Arthur Welty, William W West

Ballads of the Bivouac and the Border

Edwin Arthur Welty, William W West

Ballads of the Bivouac and the Border

ISBN/EAN: 9783744797863

Printed in Europe, USA, Canada, Australia, Japan

Cover: Foto ©Thomas Meinert / pixelio.de

More available books at **www.hansebooks.com**

Ballads of the Bivouac and the Border

⋅ by ⋅

Edwin Arthur Welty

With Introduction by Colonel William W. West, of Philadelphia.

Illustrated by Capt. J. M. Bagley, Artist of the State Historical Society of Colorado.

THE PETER PAUL BOOK COMPANY
BUFFALO
1896

Yours very Truly,
Edwin A. Helm.

To

My Mother

Mrs. Elizabeth Lehmer Zook
of St. Joseph, Missouri,

This volume
is affectionately inscribed
by her Son, the
Author

INTRODUCTION.

In 1876, while in New York, through the courtesy of the lamented
Henry Morford, then editor of the *Aldine*, I first read in manuscript
Edwin A. Welty's thrilling ballad, "The Trapper at Bay," so bold
its conception, so strong and vivid its story, so smooth and
flowing its metre, that it stamped its author at once as a master of
his chosen style of composition ; and in fancy I pictured the author,
capable of writing a ballad such as the one in question, to be
certainly a man beyond the meridian of life. Imagine my surprise
twelve years later while attending the National Republican Convention at Chicago in June, 1888, on receiving an introduction to Mr.
Welty—then a delegate from the Fourth Congressional District of
Missouri to the National Convention—to find him a young man of
scarce thirty-four years of age instead of the grizzled veteran I
had expected to greet. Such was my introduction to the distinguished author of that really great series of ballads opening with
"The Trapper at Bay" and closing with "The Huron's Answer,"
and a few details of the life of the polished writer and courteous
gentleman, whose ready pen and facile brain at less than twenty-
five years of age had made him undeniably the greatest purely
ballad writer in America, will doubtless prove of more than passing
interest to the readers of these pages—a man of whose person-
ality little has been known by the general public, and one who has
seemingly been willing to allow literary ability of a pronounced and
decided order to rust within the narrow confines of a little Southern
village.

Edwin Arthur Welty was born at Canal Dover, Ohio, December
5, 1853. His father, E. Welty, was one of the leading business
men of Eastern Ohio in that day, and his mother, Elizabeth

Lehmer Welty, was a woman of superior mental ability, good education, and natural literary capacities of no common order. His father dying in 1854, and reverses of fortune following, his widowed mother removed to Missouri in 1856, and there the greater part of his life has been spent. He resided in St. Joseph until 1876 when he removed to Oregon, Mo., and has since that time been actively engaged in the business of a broker and dealer in investment securities. Mr. Welty was educated at the St. Joseph High School, taking the classical course and was graduated in 1872, delivering the valedictory, then as now, the class honor. Immediately after his graduation he spent a year in the mountains of Colorado, Utah, New Mexico, and among the Indians and border men of that day he gained the familiarity with the scenes his pen in after years so aptly described. The life of those days was a rough and rude one, but it was also an education in itself, as the continual contact with Nature in all her moods and her wildest shapes is to a young man of impressionable mind like his. Strange and weird thoughts and fancies come unconsciously into the mind on the great plains and on the lone mountain passes of the Sierras, riding hour after hour and day after day alone in those mighty solitudes through sunlight and moonlight till the spirit of Nature broods upon one, and impressions take form and being which the calmer scenes of after life never wholly eradicate. The influence of such scenes and such surroundings are shown in all of Mr. Welty's more serious compositions. His first production, "The Trapper at Bay," appeared in the *Aldine* in 1876, and was one of a series of ballads treating of forest and savage life. It was followed by "The Hollow Oak," "Old Naomen's Fate," and closing with "The Huron's Answer." These were followed by a number of military and historical ballads of a high order, "With Washington on the Delaware,"."The Battle of Guilford Court House," "The Dragoon's Sabre," "The Assault on Quebec," and that most beauiful and touching of patiotic lyrics, "In Independence Hall." Mr. Welty is an American to the core, a lover of his country and its traditions, and his fancy glows with the ardent patriotism reflected in his historical compositions. His productions are bold, dashing and brilliant ; a master of metre, he blends with it the story teller's magic art, and is equally at home in the forest, the saddle or the battle field. He has truly the touch of genius and stands undoubtedly the foremost ballad writer in America today, and merits indeed the glowing eulogy passed upon him by Mrs. General John A. Logan on reading the graceful tribute paid to her gallant husband's valor by Mr. Welty in "The Dragoon's Sabre." In his forest legends you forget the blooming orchards and ripening grain of civilization, and see the stars at night and the sunshine of an earlier day, hear the whispering of the leaves, and the rustle of the grass and the murmur of the waters, and perhaps dream that there are other peaks of Darien besides those the awed Spaniard first gazed from in a new and unknown continent. In his border ballads you see the bivouac at night, the sweep of mighty rivers, and the legends of a fast departing race, see the wigwams dot the valleys and the fierce tribesmen's council fires, meet the braves upon the war-path and the panther in his lair. In his military and historical ballads you camp with Washington at Valley Forge, see Brandywine and Princeton, scale Quebec's Heights with Arnold, ride with Mad Anthony Wayne on the Maumee and charge with John A. Logan on the day McPherson fell. You see the sweeping columns and all of war's grand pageantry, the rattle of the old time flint lock, the roar of cannon, the shock of contending squadrons, the ring of cold steel and the clash of sabres as they cross, and if the Anglo-Saxon or the Viking spirit dwells within your breast, or the soldier's warm blood courses through your veins, you will echo what another has already well said :

> " He who rides with Welty's troopers
> Sits a steed that carries well."

The perusal of these poems would naturally lead the reader to think their author more used to the call of "boots and saddles" than the gentler thoughts that women love ; but the hand that wields the sword so well can turn a graceful compliment to a sweetheart fair, with all the ardor of a Lovelace, and is fully as much at ease in my lady's boudoir as in the shock of the foray and among bearded men at arms, as witness " The Cavalier's Toast," "Adele," "The

Rose and Bessie's Picture," and "The Rhyme of the Wedding Ring." His last poems, " The Poet's Vision " and "A New Year Greeting," are poems keyed to a minor and sadder strain than are his usual productions. These shorter poems are however, all gems of their kind, and show the versatility and real poetic genius of their author, faultless in metre and graceful in style, and yet strong and polished as they are, they are but his minor poems. It is, however, by his ballads that Mr. Welty's capacity as a writer must be judged, and the verdict of posterity as to his place as a poet must be based upon his more serious compositions, and so based, we feel the conclusion that this verdict will be, that of the younger generation of American poets, those of the period between the '70s and the '90s he has indeed had few peers and certainly no superiors.

That the fugitive and scattered sheaves of rhyme, extending over a long period of years and through the different pages of many magazines and periodicals have at last been gathered into one little volume, will be a source of great pleasure to all true lovers of verse, and prove a lasting tribute to the genius of their author, enhanced as they are by a series of striking illustrations from the pencil of the old time friend and comrade of his youth, Capt. J. M. Bagley, the distinguished artist of the State Historical Society of Colorado.

WILLIAM W. WEST.

Philadelphia, Pennsylvania.

CONTENTS.

THE TRAPPER AT BAY.

A BALLAD OF THE CANNON-BALL RIVER.

'TWAS a bleak and chilly evening, and the sun around me
    cast
Lurid shadows, the forerunners of a stormy, wintry blast.

I had spent the day in hunting, and had wandered from the
    train,
Till of it I'd lost all traces and my searching was in vain ;

Long I looked for trace of wagon o'er the prairie's withered
    sod,
Or the deeply beaten footprints of the horses, freshly shod.

I had read in books of woodcraft, that when lost on prairie
    wide,
Hunters gave their horses free rein, knowing they could
    better guide ;

So I slackened my Gray's bridle, giving him a loosened rein,
Trusting that he yet might guide me to the far-off, missing
    train.

Hardly had a mile been traversed by my worn and wearied
    steed,
Till the baying of a wolf-dog quickened him to better speed.

By a rough and rugged ravine, in a narrow, wooded glen,
Stood the rude, ungainly lodges of a band of the Cheyenne,

I was given hearty greeting by the Chieftain of the band,
While a fire, that was smoldering, soon into a blaze was
  fanned ;

Then a supper was prepared me, and was served upon the
  ground,
While the darkness, growing greater, threw its shades on
  those around.

Soon they fell to telling stories, stories of the chase and
  fight,
Of fierce charges, of brave warriors, of the wild attack at
  night ;

Thus with many a weird, wild story did the evening wear
  away,
Till a young and stalwart warrior turned to where an old
  man lay :

"Wamasego ! you have listened to these tales of warrior lore,
'Tis but fair that you should give us one from out your well-
  filled store."

Thus appealed to, rose the old man, filled his pipe again to
  smoke,
Closer round him drew his blanket, looked about him, and
  thus spoke :

" I was out upon the war-path seven and thirty years ago,
Ere the forest trees had leafed yet, or the mountains shed
their snow,

"We were thirteen active warriors, bravest young men in the
band,
Who had fought the bear and panther and the white man
hand to hand,

" We had heard from roving Pawnees that two trappers had
been seen,
Where the Cannon-Ball's swift waters join Missouri's turbid
green,

"Thither then our course was taken, and ere yet 'twas fairly
day,
We were close upon the camp-fire, where the trappers sleeping lay,

" Near them tethered stood two horses, one a chestnut, one a
bay,
And, as stealthily we neared them, suddenly we heard them
neigh ;

" Scarcely was the silence broken, ere the trappers rising fast,
Reached their horses, cut their tethers, and upon them saddles cast,

" But before the taller rider could into his saddle bound,
He was stricken by our bullets, and sank bleeding to the
ground ;

" Like the panther of the forest, leaped a warrior on his foe,
Sank a Cheyenne's heavy hatchet on the prostrate form below,

"Flashed a knife-blade in the sunlight, then the warrior's
    prize was won
And the scalp-lock of the white man flaunted from the belt of
    one;

"Leaped the other on his charger, bullets whizzing on his
    track,
While behind scarce fifty paces rode our maddened, angry
    pack;

" Rising quickly in his saddle, on my comrade bead he drew,
And the bullet from his rifle pierced his skull-bone through
    and through;

" Then we onward pressed our horses, urging them to better
    speed,
For we saw that we were gaining fast upon his jaded steed;

"Again loading on a gallop, he once more upon us wheeled,
And beneath his deadly rifle, yet another warrior reeled.

"We had reached a gentle valley,set the hills and peaks amid,
Where 'twas said by older warriors that a cave somewhere was
    hid;

" Suddenly we saw the trapper swing from out his saddle
    clear,
And toward a rocky opening, run with swiftness of a deer.

" 'Twas a dark and narrow fissure, o'er it bushes growing fast,
But he tossed aside their branches, and within its opening
passed.

" We had fired at the white man, as he disappeared from
view,
But the distance was deceptive, and our aim was far from
true ;

" Then we raised a shout of triumph, for we felt he was at
bay,
Just as shrieks the wanton eagle when he darts upon his
prey.

" While my ten companions entered, I was left to guard
without,
For we feared he might elude us by some secret passage out ;

" Scarce had my companions left me, when I saw a vivid
flash,
Followed in less than a moment by a stunning, deafening
crash ;

" Though the smoke was dense and blinding, I had soon my
entrance made,
When my senses shrank in horror from the sight therein dis-
played.

" 'Twas a sickening mass I saw there torn and mangled on
the ground,
While the heads and arms of warriors lay among the rocks
around ;

" Then I knew that the two trappers had the cave as a cache*
  used,
And, to guard against all danger, had their buried powder
  fused,

"And as soon as my companions stepped upon the hidden
  vein,
He had lit the fuse connecting, and had fired the deadly
  train.

" I had turned an abrupt angle, where the cave ran further
  back,
When the trapper stood before me to dispute my onward
  track,

" He had dropped his heavy rifle, shattered at its silvered
  stock,
And his face was torn and bleeding from the powder's sudden
  shock,

" His beard was burnt and blackened, and his teeth were
  clenched and set,
In his hand he held a bowie, and its blade with blood was
  wet,

" Looked I once upon his features, and my blood froze cold
  with fright,
Then I headlong fled before him, and betook myself to flight,

---

* Cache—a term used among the trappers and hunters of the far west, meaning a
place where furs, powder and other stores were concealed.

THE TRAPPER AT BAY.

Page 16.

"Rode I at my swiftest gallop toward the distant Cheyenne
camp,
And I never checked my charger till the grass with dew was
damp.

"I have fought in thirty battles, ne'er at danger have I
quailed,
Till that morning with the trapper, when my courage truly
failed;

"I have met your stoutest soldiers on the mountain, hill and
plain,
And within the leafy forest, I in ambuscade have lain,

"When the echoes of your volleys woke the woodland far and
near,
And the terror-stricken roe-buck from its covert fled in fear;

"When your solid, compact columns swept along an angry
flood,
And the cracking of our rifles marked their onward course
with blood;

"When the blue line of your horsemen met the swarthy line
of ours,
And the thunder of your cannon shook the trembling ground
for hours;

"At Chatuga's field I battled, when the Creeks stern Jackson
met,
When the tomahawk and war-club clashed with sword and
bayonet;

" I was under fierce old Red-Knife at the crossing of the
    Loup,
When that brave and gallant warrior fought Kit Carson and
    his troop ;

"All these scenes of blood and carnage I would gladly meet
    again,
Sooner than to face that trapper in his ghastly mountain den."

THE BATTLE OF GUILFORD COURT-HOUSE.

A BALLAD OF THE CAROLINAS.

PILE on the sticks of maple-wood, I love their ruddy glow,
'Tis only by the fireside's light that old time tales do
flow;
Thus spoke my aged Grandsire, and I seem to see him now,
While the red light of the fire falls upon his whitened brow.
His form, now bent and shrunken, had been cast in iron mold,
Though the storms of eighty winters had on limb and feature
told.

His eyes, the only feature the years had spared to him,
For the fire that blazed within them age could not quench nor
dim.
There was that about his bearing which told of earlier days,
Perhaps his homespun garments, or his quaint, old fashioned
ways.
'Twas said that Harvey Campbell full thirteen scars could show,
That his breast was scarred and broken by a stalwart red-coat's
blow.

And of all his stout companions few had borne themselves so
well,
And of siege and scout and action, few more stirring tales
could tell.

He had fought in twenty battles 'gainst the soldiers of the
    Crown,
And at Sullivan with Moultrie saw brave Jasper's flag shot
    down;
He had carried Morgan's colors at the Cow-pens bloody fight,
And was there with Wayne's battalions through Paoli's stormy
    night.

This my Grandsire, Harvey Campbell, as the past brings him
    to view,
Do you wonder that the children closer round his arm-chair
    drew?
He had promised us a story at the closing of the day,
When the dishes on the dresser had been washed and cleared
    away.
'Twas a gay and merry party at the farm-house fire that night,
Few the hearth-stones that are given such a fair and pleasant
    sight.

There was Jane, myself and Reuben, country bred, and strong
    and brown,
And our cousins, Will and Nellie, from the far off, distant town;
We were grouped about his arm-chair, wondering what the tale
    would be,
With the gentle, fair-haired Nellie perched upon her Grandpa's
    knee;
He smoothed the golden tresses, her hair was tangled wild,
Of all those gathered round him, she was e'er his favorite child.

Shall I speak of Stark or Mercer, or of Eutaw's sullen fray,
Would you hear of Quebec's fortress, or of Princeton's gallant
    day?

Not of Stark, Quebec or Mercer, tell me, Grandpa dear,
    to-night
How you fought in Carolina, at the Guilford Court-House
    fight.
Well! well! my little Nellie, then the stirring tale I'll tell,
How at Guilford that March morning, Tarleton's troopers on
    us fell.

Our watch-fires gleamed on hill and plain, as dawned the
    morning gray,
The mists that line the distant swamp in clouds are rolled away ;
The North Carolina levies with Butler's guns in train,
And Lee's three hundred riflemen hold Guilford's level plain ;
The Maryland battalion, with stout Stevens at their head,
Within the wood, beneath the slope, their bivouac has spread ;

The tents of Green's provincials dot the hill-sides in the rear,
While Washington's brave cavalry on the flanks of Greene
    appear.
There came a score of sharp reports beyond yon stretch of pine,
And, like the hail before the gale, is swept our picket line.
Lee's riflemen the coming tide in vain have tried to stem,
A troop of Tarleton's cavalry ride swiftly over them.

Scarce were the raw militia in column fairly formed,
Till at the point of bayonet their camp by Stuart was stormed,
They fired a single volley, then in hot confusion fled,
While the advancing grenadiers on Steven's line are led,
They met a raking fire from his batteries in the wood,
Twice staggered back O'Hara's men, twice was their charge
    withstood.

Again the glitter of cold steel, then Lawton's guns are lost,
The discipline of veterans tells to our raw levies cost;
Backward brave Steven's men are hurled by yonder line of
    steel,
Toward the long slope held by Greene the broken column reel,
The shakos of the grenadiers press onward up the slope,
To crush the center of our line was now O'Hara's hope.

From wood, and slope and thicket, our volleys fiercely broke,
Men fell before it like the grain 'neath lusty mower's stroke,
The veterans of Cornwallis keep step to tap of drum,
The officers cheer on the men, the colors nearer come,
Their volleys faint and fainter grew, we wondered at the lull,
Ere lifted from before our sight, the smoke-cloud gray and
    dull.

When suddenly to listening ear a trampling sound is heard,
The soul of every trooper then with eagerness is stirred,
The English Guard is forming, is whispered down the line,
If any man felt terror then he showed no outward sign ;
We heard a cheer the silence break and echo down the flanks,
And General Greene and Washington rode slowly down the
    ranks.

They halted by our battery, Greene tossed aside his cloak,
And facing now our eager men, these were the words he
    spoke :
"Men of the South! I ask you prove the strength of field
    and forges,
As you in shock of battle meet the red-coats of the Georges,
Remember Tarleton's quarter, he who never spared a foe,
And on the field of Guilford strike for man and home a blow."

A moment more, and on our right, their charging columns
    drift,
And now a mass of scarlet breaks the sullen smoke-clouds rift,
We thought of Buford's cruel death, of gray-haired mothers
    spurned,
Of homes destroyed, of fields laid waste, of cot and hamlet
    burned,
How Tarleton's course was ever marked by dark and crimson
    stains,
And, at the thought, a thrill of hate surged hotly through our
    veins.

They little dream, that iron troop, who charge o'er Guilford's
    heath,
That full two hundred of the Guard ride to a trooper's death;
Then came a noise like thunder, we feel a sudden shock,
The granite of the old world's hills has met the new world's
    rock;
A moment and they falter, the British ranks are cleft,
As by a stroke of lightning the stricken clouds are reft.

But hark ! above the battle's din is borne a startling cry,
And as our bleeding squadrons wheel, a wild sight meets the
    eye.
A troop of Tarleton's iron men through our frail line had
    pressed,
And at a swinging gallop rode towards a knoll's sharp crest,
No need to tell why 'gainst that point surged yonder human
    storm,
For boldly outlined on its brow we traced our General's form.

Around him scarce a dozen men. God save that gallant
      group !
For fifty soldiers of the King ride in the coming troop,
With reins tight held and rowels sunk I wheeled my panting
      steed,
And with a score of troopers rode, urged by our General's
      need ;
A moment more, and as the winds o'er Guilford's hillsides
      sweep,
So do a score of trusty blades from ringing scabbards leap.

I saw upon a chestnut horse a Colonel of the Guard,
As with a file of fierce dragoons, he pressed our General hard,
Full well I know the officer who rides the chestnut horse,
He must know how to wield a sword, who blades with Stuart
      would cross,
He saw the peril in his rear, and quickly on us wheeled,
Beneath Stuart's thrust a comrade near soon in his saddle
      reeled.

He came upon me with an oath, I parried his fierce blow,
And with a well directed stroke, I laid the trooper low ;
A pistol flashed before my face, I felt a stinging pain,
And oozing down my saddle bow came crimson drops of rain,
My reins dropped nerveless, and I fell unconscious from my
      horse,
And there was by my comrades found, prone on the Colonel's
      corse.

I woke to find Nathaniel Greene a watcher at my bed,
"You did your duty well today," he gravely to me said,

But added as he water held, for my hot lips to quaff,
"And he who wields so true a blade shall ride on Greene's
    own staff,
And let whate'er this soldier needs from my own tent be
    sent,"
Then bowing to the surgeons there, he rose and left the tent.

My Grandsire's tale was finished, shadows had o'er wainscot
    crept,
And with head on Grandpa's shoulder, little Nellie long had
    slept,
Shone the hearth-fire's dying embers o'er the children's faces
    bright,
And on veteran of Guilford fell a benison of light.
Long the children sat in silence, misting eyes their language
    spoke,
Till the sturdy voice of Willie thus upon the silence broke:

"Grandpa, will e'er the King again for conquest seek our
    land?
If so myself and Reuben will like you at Guilford stand."
"Fitly spoken, little Grandson, you would do your part, I
    know,
But the land that bears such spirits need not fear a foreign foe,
Ne'er will fleet of Howe or Carleton in the future seek our
    shore,
And the cruel men of Tarleton ne'er will ride on Guilford
    more."

THE HOLLOW OAK.

A LEGEND OF ST. CLAIR'S DEFEAT.

I.

WHERE the peaks of the Sierras
    Melt into an endless blue,
And the San Juan's fierce current
    Bursts upon the startled view ;

Where the dashing mountain torrents
    Through the misty gorges gleam,
And the cañon's surging waters
    Join the river's swollen stream ;

Where the tall and tapering pine trees
    Rear their crests towards the skies,
And the snow upon the mountains
    In its dazzling whiteness lies ;

There, beneath the threatening shadow
    Of a high, o'erhanging peak,
Stood a cabin, which a trapper
    Built there from some sudden freak.

It was made of heavy pine logs,
    From the forest cut away,
While the cracks and interstices
    Had been chinked with yellow clay;

In one corner stood a fire-place,
    O'er it hooks for rifles hung,
While beneath, a grimy camp-kettle
    From its heavy handle swung;

On the hearth a glowing fire
    Crackled with a merry sound,
Lighting up the sun-browned faces
    Of the trappers grouped around.

They had gathered at the cabin,
    As night's shadows darker grew,
For the place had long been noted
    As a hunters' rendezvous;

Some were burnishing their rifles,
    Others filling pouch and horn,
Wishing to be up and ready
    For an early start at morn.

Thus engaged, they soon were telling
    Stories of their earlier days,
Such as only have their being
    In the wild frontiersmen's lays:

Of the chapparal and prairie,
    Of some daring deed well done,
How the panther had been hunted,
    Or some hard fought battle won ;

Of the fierce and bloody savage,
    And the still more bloody aid,
Which he found upon the border
    In the reckless renegade.

Each in turn had told some story
    Of the forest and the chase—
All, save one, a gray, old trapper,
    Sitting from the rest apace.

Silence fell upon the circle,
    All sat quiet—no one spoke :
Then the old man laid his pipe down,
    And he thus the silence broke :

" Near the towns of the Miami,
    With my brother I was there,
When St. Clair's ill-fated legions
    Fell into the Mohawk's * snare ;

" When the war-whoop of the savage
    Rang throughout the forest glade,
Blanching cheeks, whose ruddy color
    Had ne'er known a paler shade ;

---

* Until the year 1838 it was generally conceded that Little Turtle commanded the Indians at the time of St. Clair's defeat. But Mr. Stone, in his life of Brandt, the celebrated Mohawk, claims that he led the Indians that day. Be the truth as it may, it will probably always be a disputed point, and one never satisfactorily determined.

" When from every tree and thicket
Dashed and poured a deadly rain,
And the keen and well-aimed hatchet
Pierced the warm and quivering brain.

" Through the whole of that dread conflict
Fought we stoutly, side by side,
Till the grass around was watered
By a dark and crimson tide.

" Fell our comrades fast around us,
And we saw 't would be in vain
Now to urge our shattered columns
'Gainst their hidden foe again.

" Fled we then with hurried footsteps
Through the forest's leafy dale,
While a score of angry Shawnees
Followed on our fresh-made trail.

" We were weary and exhausted
By the morning's bloody fight,
And we knew that they were gaining
Fast upon us in our flight.

" We had neared an old oak, stricken
By the lightning's ruthless blast,
And its leafless, withered branches
Round about the ground were cast.

" Turned my brother to me quickly,
    And he said : ' Were it not best
That we part ! for by so doing
    Each may be less hotly pressed ? '

" I assented ; and we parted,
    Promising, whate'er befell,
We would meet upon the morrow
    At a spot we both knew well.

" Plunged I deeper in the forest,
    With its many dangers fraught,
Till I'd baffled my pursuers,
    When the rendezvous I sought.

" There I waited for my brother
    All that long and dreary day,
Trusting that he yet might join me,
    Or perhaps had missed his way ;

" But he came not there to meet me,
    And my fears upon me grew,
So I thought, that to dispel them
    I would search the woodland through.

" Then with quick and wary footsteps
    Threaded I the lonely wood,
While the gaunt and hungry gray-wolf
    Wandering on my pathway stood.

" Over muskets, broken sword hilts,
  And the mangled heaps of slain,
Searched I long to find his body,
  Or at least some clue to gain.

"Days I hunted in the forest
  Some poor trace of him to find ;
But at last all hope had left me,
  And I then my search resigned.

II.

" Years had passed ; and I was clearing
  Off a narrow strip of wood ;
For I wished to place my cabin
  Where the forest trees then stood.

" One by one the leafy giants
  Bowed beneath my axe's stroke,
Till at length all lay before me,
  Save a hollow, shattered oak.

" 'Twas the old oak I had noticed
  On that wild night years before,
When I, panting, fled the Shawnees
  From Miami's field of gore ;

" Thoughtfully I gazed upon it ;
  Then my axe swung high and well,
Till it swayed awhile, and tottering,
  At my very feet it fell.

" When it fell, it burst asunder,
    And exposed some bones to sight,
While a ring, of curious setting,
    Flashed and sparkled in the light.

" 'Twas my brother's ring I saw there—
    Then I knew his awful doom ;
For he must have died of hunger
    In that narrow, living tomb !

" He had doubtless entered, hoping
    To elude his savage foe,
And was fastened, starving, dying,
    In the gloomy depths below ;

" Gathered I the crumbling fragments,
    Then a grave for them I made ;
And beneath a spreading chestnut
    My poor brother's bones I laid.''

He had finished ; and the teardrops
    Stole o'er many a hardened face,
That perhaps since early childhood,
    Ne'er had felt such tender grace.

THE ASSAULT ON QUEBEC.

DECEMBER 31, 1775. A BALLAD OF THE NORTH.

I FEEL the crisp October breeze sweep o'er the Laurel Hill,
The scent of clover in the fields comes to my nostrils
still.

Above, a distant eagle floats majestic in the sky,
And from the copse a flock of quail, loud whirring, scurry by.

A dew drop twinkles on each leaf and tiny blade of grass,
The laurel on each mountain slope wears now a crimson mass.

I take my milking pail in hand, my morning tasks to do,
And in the east the early light shows yet a star or two.

Slow at my call the patient cows come grazing down the lane,
When suddenly at pasture bars a horseman draws his rein.

The fleck of foam upon his bit tells of the rider's pace,
Few were the men could saddle sit with Jacob Lehmer's grace.

" Good morning, Cousin Jacob; why so early ride today?
Methought you at your father's house full thirty miles away."

The opening scene of this ballad is located at the site of the old homestead of the
author's mother in the mountains of Somerset County, Pennsylvania, on the slopes
of the Laurel Hill, a spur of the Alleghanies.

35

"I rode last night from Bedford Springs, I left its Inn at ten,
Tonight I join at Carrick's Ford a troop of Morgan's men.

"John Frease! you come of lineage such as ne'er at danger
    quail,
That sinewy arm can better wield a sword than milking pail.

" Why stay you idle on this farm ?   Aside your plough-share
    lay.
Come join the men that Arnold leads to bring the foe to bay.

" Montgomery with a thousand men sweeps scon o'er Lake
    Champlain,
While Arnold's stout New England troops push through the
    woods of Maine.

" Together joined the two commands will crush the startled foe,
And on the heights of Quebec strike a fell, decisive blow.

"I ask you prove no laggard, John, meet us at Carrick's
    Ford."
At this he turned his panting steed, but said no other word.

I felt the blood in every vein in swifter current stir,
A longing fierce swept o'er me, but—my mother, what of her?

I left my pail beside the bars and backward took my way,
A moment more within the door I met my mother gray.

" What brings you back so soon, my son, the dawn is scarce
    in sight,
Surely the milking of the cows is not a task so light."

" Mother, the die at last is cast.   I leave your side today.
You have a man beside you now, and not a child at play.

" I cannot till these peaceful fields until war's work is done,
He who would shirk his country's call is not a worthy son."

"Stay, John," she whispered in my ear, "the winter storms
    draw near,
And on these laurelled mountain sides lurk dangers women
    fear.

" 'Twas only yesterday I heard a Mingo's track was seen,
Where yonder valley near the ford lies clothed in peaceful
    green.

" 'Tis said a band of Tories come to pillage, burn and loot,
And with the Mingoes in their train sweep down the Turkey-
    foot.

" My son," my mother trembling said, " I pray you do not go,
My heart already sore is rent, spare me this final blow."

Two sons bear muskets in the ranks with Sullivan and Darke.
The eldest, Henry, rides an aid upon the staff of Stark.

I seized my mother's trembling hand.   " No son could love
    you more,
But I must with my brothers stand ; your blessing I implore.

"You know the blood of Michael Frease flows hotly in my veins,
Men of that race have never bent their limbs to tyrant's
    chains."

I see the tear-drops trickle down my mother's upturned face,
Years had not robbed its features of a trace of girlish grace.

She spoke no word, but rising took from off the mantle-piece
The sword that once on Braddock's field was won by Michael
Frease.

" Take this, 't is all I have to give, remember how 'twas won,
Your father, dying, left his sword to you his youngest son.

"Go bear yourself in field and fight a Pennsylvanian's son,
And come not back unto this hearth till liberty be won."

I met at Carrick's Ford that night a score of men or more,
Clad in the home-made buckskin suits that Morgan's men all
wore.

Virginians true from Shepherdstown and men from Delaware,
But most of those who bivouacked there stout Pennsylvanians
were.

At morn we eastward took our way to join the main command,
That through the Northern wilderness bold Arnold led by
land.

How chafed that lion-hearted man beneath the wintry sky,
When faint from cold and want of food the bravest sink and
die ;

How everywhere the General went to cheer the struggling
men,
Put on his horse a wounded man and would not mount again.

At last the march was at an end—the river came in sight,
And Quebec's frowning citadel loomed upward on our right ;

Upon those bleak, Canadian plains stretch tents in white
array,
Around the fortress 'neath whose walls the foe beleaguered
lay.

We with Montgomery pitch our tents and watch the wary foe.
Days lengthened into weary weeks—and yet is struck no blow.

In vain were sorties daily made as fowlers spread their nets.
The wily foe could not be lured beyond stone parapets.

Unused to Northern winters, harassed by cold and snow,
Wearied by sheer inaction, the army's murmurs grow.

Restless and irksome sped the days to all in camp alike,
We longed for clash of battle—the time had come to strike.

Montgomery then decided in two commands to form,
And at the bayonet's keen point take Quebec's Heights by
storm.

His own New York battalions should charge the upper town,
While Arnold's troops and Morgan's men should sweep St.
John's gates down.

Next morning, ere the rising sun above the Heights appears,
The booming of Montgomery's guns comes faintly to our ears.

A moment more and up the slope our charging column sweeps,
And from the walls above our heads a wave of fire leaps.

A volley fierce of musketry has ploughed our charging ranks,
Men fall like trees before a storm in center, rear and flanks.

I hear a whizzing, singing noise, 't was made by cannon ball,
And on the slope behind me note a horse and rider fall.

I felt a shudder o'er me creep, a feeling 'kin to fear,
The Pennsylvania mountain lad had ne'er seen death so near.

As on the column swiftly moves I see a well-known form,
His bearing firm, his stalwart breast bared to the leaden storm.

'Twas Jacob Lehmer's figure, his form erect and straight,
The first to reach St. John's gray walls, the first to scale its
    gate ;

The grim redoubt is taken, the British backward fell,
And closely pressed take refuge within the citadel.

Again the roar of shotted guns, the British cannoneer
Within the ranks of charging men has mowed a pathway clear.

I saw my cousin backward reel, his hand upon his heart,
A fleck of blood is on his lips, his nostrils wide apart.

I sprang to aid the stricken man, his head falls on my breast—
The gallant comrade of my youth lies dead on Quebec's crest.

THE CHARGE ON ST. JOHN'S GATE, QUEBEC.

Page 40.

I closed my kinsman's glazing eyes, the heart that knew no
    fear,
When came the clash of backwoodsman 'gainst British
    grenadier.

I felt my heart with anguish start, my veins surge hot with
    hate,
The blood of every red-coat there could not my passion sate ;

I lost no time, but in the charge press on with Morgan's men,
I felt no fear of mortal foe and scorned all danger then.

The redoubts blaze with musketry, its cannon speak their ire,
The charging column sways and fades like grass 'neath prairie
    fire.

Backward the storming column is hurled down Quebec's slope.
Muscle and blood, howe'er well spent, cannot with bastion
    cope.

Again is formed the broken line with Arnold at their head,
Against the citadel's proud gates the bleeding ranks are led.

The remnant left of Morgan's men in squads of ten are toled,
And two men of each charging squad stout scaling ladders
    hold ;

Again we face their musketry, again their cannon spoke,
The ground is wet with crimson stains, the air is black with
    smoke ;

The line sweeps onward with a rush—some ladders reach the wall,
Those who assay to mount their rungs beneath them lifeless fall.

I hear brave Arnold cheer his men, his voice rang loud and clear,
"Take yonder citadel's proud flag, or leave your General here."

His sword was broken at its hilt, his blazing eyes were set,
Where float the British colors high on yonder parapet.

He grasped a scaling ladder and up it lightly swung,
Aud twixt the earth and parapet a moment only hung.

His form above the bastion rose, so quickly was it done,
To those below it seemed as if the bastion had been won.

Then came a cannon's dull report, a hurtling shower of ball,
Swept from the parapet's support, both man and ladder fall;

I seize the wounded officer and stagger down the slope,
Bleeding with wounds and faintness at times my way I grope

Over the dead and dying with my burden firmly grasped,
While the stiffening arms of Arnold around me tight are clasped.

Faintly I hear the clash of steel, the cannon's sullen roar,
At last the slope behind me lies—and then I know no more.

Bleeding, and torn and mangled, I swooned upon the ground,
But, shielding yet the General, by kindly hands was found.

For hours I lay unheeding, but at last I conscious woke,
The regimental surgeon with his hand on mine thus spoke :

" Young man ! your gallant action saved Arnold's life today,
And he, though sorely wounded, bids me at your bedside stay.

" He sends you cordial greetings, and bids me to you state,
John Frease's first commission from Quebec's Heights will
    date."

Three months of weary waiting 'neath the surgeon's skillful
    hand,
Then I, pallid, wan and wasted joined Schuyler's brave
    command.

I fought at Saratoga's field, when Burgoyne's sword was won,
And at the charge on Stony Point was not the hindmost one;

At Germantown and Monmouth, a Colonel of Dragoons,
I met with Wayne's battalions, Knyphausen's grim platoons ;

I saw King George's colors furled on Yorktown's last redoubt,
As slow the British regulars in silence march without.

To Washington's headquarters, then, I went at close of day,
And with a furlough granted, quickly northward took my
    way.

No longer beardless stripling, but a soldier to the core,
Little to mark the conntry lad but the good sword which he
    wore.

Again I slept at Carrick's Ford, and long ere dawn was red,
I reached the old familiar road that up the valley led,

And as the Ford was left behind my swift gray's iron hoof,
I saw behind the meadows rise the old-time country roof.

I halted at the pasture bars and tied my horse's rein,
And with a quickened footstep tread the winding, grassy lane.

Then wide I swung the picket gate that led to cottage door,
A moment more, with beating heart, I crossed its threshold
    o'er.

I heard a faint and smothered cry, of joy and not alarm,
My mother's slender figure lay within her son's strong arm.

I saw a thrill of conscious pride sweep o'er my mother's face,
As on my dusty epaulets she saw the colonel's lace.   .

I told her how in battle fierce my chevrons first were won,
Her eyes were wet with falling tears long ere my tale was
    done.

Then slowly rising said, as she the sword took from my waist,
" 'Tis fitting that in times of peace your sword be better
    placed."

And added, as the blade she hung above the mantle-piece,
" I see you bore it as becomes a son of Michael Frease."

She told me much in broken words, bent was she now and
gray,
But of my kindred spoke no words—my brothers, where were
they?

She answered not, but rising said, " My son, pray follow me.
He who at Quebec proved his blood, his father's grave should
see."

She led me to a grassy mound beyond the hillsides' crest,
Where underneath an arching oak he sleeps in peaceful rest,

And on the Laurel Hill's soft slope three headstones new I
mark—
The sons who fought with Sullivan and him who rode with
Stark.

TO NELLIE.

A NEW YEAR GREETING JANUARY 1, 1884.

THE clock is ticking on the stand, the hands point now
    at one,
The New Year halts on Time's threshold, and '83 is done;
A fitting time and place, I ween, for retrospection's play,
And thirty years are sure enough to cool hot passion's sway.
Aha, my love, I know you'll say five years of wedlock's chains
Has chilled the current that once flowed so hotly through my
    veins.

Not so, my dear.   I call on him who o'er my shoulder peers,
The glad New Year just ushered in, ere Time his vision seers,
True answer to my question give, does not the heart you see
In every throb beat staunch and fond allegiance unto thee?
He nods his head in mute reply my Nellie's charms have quite
Sufficed to take his breath away as well as dazzle sight.

Nay, can you wonder, sweetheart mine, you hold me bound
    so fast,
When even o'er immortals you can your witchery cast?
I start, my sight seems strangely dim, I glance around the room,
Naught greets me save the embers bright, whose flashes break
    the gloom.
But, be it dream or fancy, whate'er the vision dear,
To her I love, my Nellie sweet, a happy, glad New Year.

THE CAVALIER'S TOAST.

I.

FILL up your glasses, comrades, fill to the very brim,
    I would give as a toast a woman, a woman neat and
    trim,
Let your glasses clink till their echoes ring,
While a garland of song at her feet I fling.

II.

Can you picture the graces of motion, set to a form divine,
Eyes whose brilliancy rivals the sparkle and glitter of wine,
Lips like the rubies of Ophir, meeting o'er teeth of pearl,
Such as lie in the depths of ocean, where the maddening
    eddies whirl.

III.

A brow as fair as the lily that droops ere the day is done,
A smile as warm as the roses that bloom 'neath a tropical sun,
And a voice, ever musical, gentle and low,
As the soft, fabled breezes, which o'er Araby blow.

IV.

Ah ! you pause with your glasses lifted—each others eyes you
    seek,
You would know the name of this houri, of this angel so to
    speak ;
Drain, drain your glasses, my comrades ! her name on my lips
    is rife,
'Tis the sweetest name known to woman—'tis that of my
    loving wife.

THE DRAGOON'S SABRE.

A BALLAD OF THE DAY MC PHERSON FELL.

IN a quaint, New England village, where tall maples line the
   street,
'Neath whose leaves, the June day's sunshine falls a molten,
   glimmering sheet ;
Where the Kennebec's soft waters sweep along, a silver thread,
Through whose meadows, rich with clover, lowing herds are
   daily led ;

There beneath a maple's shadow, stood a homestead, old and
   gray,
While o'er windows, door and casement climbing vines in
   clusters stray;
And within the open doorway struggling sunbeams softly fall,
Till they touch a dragoon's sabre hanging on the further wall.

Gleams the blade of polished metal, as the sunbeams o'er it
   roam,
Strange adornment, say you surely, for that peaceful cottage
   home.

The scene of this ballad is located in Augusta, Maine ; being suggested by an
incident occurring there at the meeting of General Logan with James G. Blaine
during the great political campaign of 1884 when Blaine and Logan were the
Republican standard bearers.

The perusal of the above ballad brought to its author, Mr. Welty, the following characteristic letter from Mrs. John A. Logan, accompanied by a striking
picture of the General.

Near the window, in an arm-chair, sits a man of iron mold,
Yet his rough and rugged outlines still showed a bearing bold.

The blood of men who fought with Knox coursed in the old
    man's veins,
He came of good Green Mountain stock, whose limbs ne'er
    bent to chains ;
And 'twas said that Andrew Warner had faced death in every
    form —
In the march, and siege, and picket, in the battle's deadliest
    storm.

He had fought at Cerro Gordo, and had charged at Monterey,
And when boomed the guns of Sumter, he was ready for the
    fray.
Under Grant, at Chattanooga, he had stormed the cloud-
    capped ridge,
And with Streight, and his bold troopers, crossed the Chatta-
    hoochee bridge;

With the Rock of Chickamauga he had stood that autumn
    day,
When the bleeding corps of Thomas held the rebel horde at
    bay.
By the veteran sat his grandchild, while he smoothed her
    tangled hair,
When the echoes of a bugle floated on the summer air ;

Followed by the boom of cannon and the tramp of many feet,
And a throng of surging people fill the old New England
    street.

"What means this?" the veteran's grandchild answering
    caught the street's glad strain,
"Why, they say that John A. Logan greets today the Man of
    Maine."

Trembling rose the aged soldier, gazed he fixedly and long
On a tall, commanding figure moving 'mid the hurrying
    throng.
Murmured he, "'tis General Logan, I would know him any-
    where,
With his grand and stalwart figure, and his courtly, martial
    air."

Fainter grew the strains of music and the tramp of hurrying
    feet,
Till at last the usual silence fell upon the village street.
Then the old man left the window, took the child upon his
    knee,
And, upon his rugged features, trace of tear-drops you could
    see.

Broke the child the solemn silence, clear her words as soft
    they fall,
"Tell me how you won the sabre hanging on the cottage
    wall.
Not of Champion Hills and Vicksburg, where you bore
    yourself so well,
Tell me how you fought with Logan on the day McPherson
    fell!"

"Why, my child, I've often told you of the sabre and the
 day;
Would you like again to listen, how was won the bloody
 fray?"
"Yes," plead the child. The veteran's face beamed on her
 soft and mild,
His lost youth's fiery spirit seemed reflected in the child.

"Well, so be it! Listen Ethel, while the stirring tale I'll
 tell,
Of the scenes that July morning when Hood's line upon us
 fell.
The night before, in Logan's tent, the battle had been
 planned,
How on the left McPherson's corps should Hood's advance
 withstand.

"The center Blair's brigades should hold, ere dawned the
 morning light,
While on the right bold Logan's men should early force the
 fight.
The bugle called at early dawn, our battle line was formed,
'Twas whispered that the breast-works near by Hood would
 soon be stormed.

"The cassions of the batteries shone black as rose the sun;
Grim cannoneers in uniform stood each beside his gun;
The bayonets of the infantry gleamed brightly rank on rank,
While the dragoons and mounted men were ranged upon the
 flank.

" The boom of Logan's heavy guns comes faintly to our ears,
When suddenly, along our front, a thread of gray appears;
Then came a crash of musketry, and then our cannon roar,
And on the swiftly moving ranks a deadly fire we pour.

" Our volleys fierce and fiercer grew, the tide of gray
rolled on,
To melt in spray, as do the waves that dash the cliffs upon.
McPherson's every nerve was strained to baffle Hood till
night,
For Blair had failed to fill the gap that opened on our right.

" Thus we fought from early sunrise and had barely held our
ground,
While the heaps of dead and dying told how fierce the fight
around.
At last their charge begins to tell, our columns sway and
rock—
The lines that stood so firm since dawn yield slightly to the
shock.

" A courier reined his panting steed where our brave colonel
stood,
And said, 'McPherson dying lies in yon narrow strip of
wood.'
So low the words you scarce would think the officer had
heard,
And yet the murmur down the ranks showed our whole line
was stirred.

JOHN A. LOGAN RALLYING THE BROKEN LINES ON THE DAY McPHERSON FELL.

Page 57.

" In vain I saw the officers appealing to the men.
No human power, you would have said, could hold them firm
    again.
A battery of heavy guns was taken on our left.
It seemed as if the wavering line in twain would soon be cleft—

" When suddenly there comes a lull, and then a burst of
    cheers,
And in that hell of death and shell the master's form appears.
A swarthy figure, powder stained, swift down the line doth
    ride,
Beneath his charger's hoofs the dust marks every swinging
    stride.

" The glittering star on shoulder bar the rider's rank showed
    well,
It needed not the wild huzzas that rent the air to tell.
'Twas Logan come in person to save the waning day,
He asked no one to follow save where he lead the way.

" ' My comrades true, your duty do, your leader's death
    avenge,
And be the charging squadron's cry, ' McPherson and
    revenge !'
Close up the ranks, in column charge, upon yon battery wheel,
Ride down those gray-clad cannoneers, give them a touch of
    steel ! '

" They hear the gallant leader's voice, the shattered ranks
    reform,
The hoarse cry rolling down the ranks forbodes the coming
    storm.

McPherson and revenge the cry, as flashed our glittering
   blades,
And at our charging column's head rode Logan and his aides.

" Full thirty double shotted guns play on the bronzed dragoons,
And good three thousand muskets sweep their grim, compact
   platoons.
Straight for the guns the columns swept, in vain the can-
   nons roar,
Fades cannoneers and infantry like chaff from threshing floor.

" My horse swept onward in the rush, my eyes were fixed
   away,
Upon a gold-laced color guard, dressed in a garb of gray.
The flag was knotted round his waist, his sword he waved
   on high,
The swath of dead about him showed he well the blade could
   ply ;

" A moment more our sabres crossed, then came the clash of
   steel,
I saw my foeman backward start, and in his saddle reel.
But child ! he was a swordsman true, his blade had grazed
   my hair,
While mine had cleft his temple through and laid his skull-
   bone bare.

" I grasped the blood-stained colors from the trooper when
   he fell,
And heard the manly Union cheer above the rebel yell.

CALUMET PLACE.
WASHINGTON, D.C.
Feb. 27/ 888

Respectfully yours,

Mrs. General Logan

'Well done, my gallant comrade,' The words rang loud and
    clear ;
I turned and saw that Logan and his staff were riding near.

" 'I wish that I full recompense for such a deed could show,
But a full-fledged Captain's epaulets will grace that form I
    know.'
He drew his sword from out his belt. 'Let this my own
    thanks tell,
I know that Captain Warner's arm this blade will e'er wield
    well.'

" I tried to thank the General, as he gave the sword to me,
But so full my eyes of joyous tears, I could neither speak nor
    see.
At last I spoke, but Logan then was dashing to the front,
His fiery spirit ne'er could rest save at the battle's brunt."

The old man stooped and kissed the child, "My dear, my
    tale is done,
I've told you how in manhood's prime yon sabre, child, was
    won."
The child looked up. The eyes that e'er gleamed fiercest in
    the fight,
Were fixed upon her upturned face with soft and tender light.

AT THIRTY-TWO.

JANUARY 1, 1886.

MEN shake me by the hand and say :
    "By Jove! old boy, you are getting gray,
There are furrowed lines upon your face,
And crow's feet under your eyes we trace,
You have aged ten years since we saw you last.
No use talking, my son, you are failing fast."
I laugh at their jesting—I turn to the glass.
There is no use denying, the truth is, a lass
At these wrinkled features would scarce deign a glance
From eyes that young hearts can pierce like a lance.
Am I then so old ? Nay, I feel it not so.
At thirty-two years hearts can yet palpably glow,
And as a sweet form on my vision arises,
I own to not the least of my many surprises.
For so rounded a figure, so trim built a waist,
The girdle of Venus herself never graced ;
And the eyes that look down in a shy, tender way,
The deuce with the toughest of heart-strings can play,
And the flush that flits lightly from temple to cheek
Whole volumes of love in a second can speak.
Away, then, with the fancy that love ever grows cold,
Though the hair may be gray, the heart never grows old,

And the alchemist's vision—Ponce De Leon's wild quest,
Your husband has found, when he clasps you to his breast,
For in Mary's fond love I have found what forsooth
Is the long searched for fount of perpetual youth.

L'ENVOI.

Oh ! Months of the New Year, to you I appeal.
On the brow of my darling set lightly your seal ;
Stop your car, Father Time, leave off your old tricks,
Deal her nothing but blessings, oh ! Year '86.

OLD NAOMEN'S FATE.

A BALLAD OF THE MINGO NATION.

GLEAMED the water in the moonlight,
  Swayed the forest in the breeze,
While the blue smoke of a camp-fire
  Curled aloft amid the trees.

Flung the fire its ruddy shadows
  On a band of men grouped near,
Such as only can be met with
  On the rude and stern frontier.

The dried pelts of bear and beaver
  Tell their calling to the sight,
For a score of roving trappers
  Had encamped there for the night.

They were brown, and bronzed, and bearded,
  Used to scenes of blood and strife ;
For upon the reckless border
  Each had spent a checkered life.

In strange contrast with the others,
  One I saw of darker cheek,
And his swarthy, beardless features
  The wild Indian blood bespeak.

He was of the Mingo Nation,
　Sole survivor of his band,
For the rest had long since perished
　By the white man's ruthless hand.

Silently he sat and listened
　To the tales his comrades wove,
Of the dangers of the forest,
　Of the men its pathways rove.

Told they, too, of the wild Indian,
　Of the traits that mark his race,
That of gratitude and pity
　You could find in him no trace.

" Hold my comrades "—and the trappers
　Started as his voice they heard,
For the Mingo, while among them,
　Had but rarely spoke a word.

" I have heard you speak this evening
　Of the red man's treachery,
That for favors kindly shown him
　He would ever faithless be.

" Have you never heard of Logan,
　How he fought with Winnemac?
How the wild and fierce Oneidas
　Hung upon the Tory's track?

" That among our savage nations
    You will find bad men, I own,
But is it among the red men
    That ingrates you find alone?

" Did the renegades you sent us
    E'er of pity teach us aught?
No ! our sternest, fiercest warriors
    Ne'er such bloody deeds have wrought.

" But I have a tale to tell you
    Of a warrior true and tried,
Who to save a friendly white man
    His own fate and tribe defied.

" Near our wigwams on the Wabash,
    Where our towns may yet be traced,
There a bold and daring settler
    Had his rude log cabin placed.

" There he dwelt in peace and safety
    In the midst of our wild band,
All unconscious of the danger
    That lurked round on every hand.

" For within his open doorway
    Our fierce warriors often came,
And ne'er wanted food or welcome
    From the settler or his dame.

" There was one among our number,
   An aged chieftain, bent and gray,
Who toward the white man's cabin
   Had been often seen to stray.

" He was honored by his people,
   And Naomen well might be,
For when young the Mingo Nation
   Had but few as bold as he.

" In fierce struggles with the white men
   No one bore a braver part,
And the warriors in the council
   He could sway with matchless art.

" Under Pontiac at Detroit,
   E'er had failed his well planned snare,
With that wily, cunning warrior
   And his Hurons he was there.

" He had fought upon the Maumee
   When the allied tribes met Wayne,
When Mad Anthony's stout troopers
   Crushed the Indians of the plain.

" There he sat and smoked for hours
   In the peaceful cabin's shade,
While before the agéd chieftain
   Food and drink were often laid.

" Thus a year or more among us
   Lived the white man and his wife,
Till the border by Tecumseh
   Was again stirred into strife.

" One by one the neighboring nations
   Runners to Tecumseh sent,
And our tribe, though seeming peaceful,
   Was yet filled with discontent.

" For 'twas whispered that the Mingoes
   Held themselves aloof from fear,
That they thought their lives and wigwams
   Than their kindred far more dear.

" So at last it was decided
   'Gainst the settlements to go,
And to sweep them from the border
   By one fell, decisive blow.

" So the morrow found me lurking
   In a thicket in the wood,
Where, within a narrow clearing,
   Stacy's rough hewn cabin stood.

" For we feared he might elude us
   And our well laid plans betray,
And escaping, warn the settlers
   Of the peril in their way.

" Soon the cabin door was opened,
    And with quick and stealthy tread,
Came the pale-faced man and woman
    And towards the river sped.

" They had looked toward the thicket,
    As they hurried on their way,
But they failed to note my presence
    As I crouching in it lay.

" Scarcely had I saw them pass me
    Ere a copse hid them from sight,
When I hastened to our village
    And gave warning of their flight.

" Near us a canoe was fastened,
    And in it we quickly leap,
And upon the flying settlers
    With a rapid stroke we sweep.

" Gained we fast upon the white man
    As his oars he swiftly plied,
Till at last he seized his rifle
    And his paddles threw aside.

" We could see the polished barrel
    Glitter in the morning's light ;
And the keen eyes of the settler
    Glance from tube to polished sight.

" Sharply rang the crack of rifle,
  Swiftly sped the deadly ball,
And the paddles of our steersman
  In the seething waters fall.

" Quickly sprang another warrior
  To the dying oarsman's place,
Not a moment's time was wasted
  In our fierce and eager chase.

" Cut our boat the foaming current
  Like the arrow from the bow,
Every stroke, though, brought us nearer
  To our half exhausted foe.

" We could see his muscles bending
  To the oars of maple wood,
While the sweat upon his forehead
  In long, quivering bead-drops stood.

" He was known upon the waters
  As an oarsman skilled and true,
But what could he, single-handed,
  Against ten strong warriors do?

" He was quickly overtaken,
  And upon the council ground,
With his pallid wife beside him,
  He was led securely bound.

" There in groups around the fire,
  In their forest costume dressed,
Sat the chief men of the nation,
  And Naomen 'mid the rest.

" They had gathered to determine
  What the prisoner's fate should be,
And in all that savage council
  None more stern and grave than he.

" Then, in turn, the whites were questioned
  As to who betrayed the band,
While a Mingo o'er each prisoner
  Stands with tomahawk in hand.

" Name the traitor or else perish,
  But they answered not a word,
Though the pale-faced woman trembled
  As their cruel fate she heard.

" 'Woman! would you have your husband
  Perish here before your eyes?
Speak, or else, by the Great Spirit!
  In his tracks the white man dies.'

" To these words there came no answer,
  But ere fell the hatchet's stroke,
On the silent, listening circle
  Old Naomen's voice thus broke :

" ' The pale face has kept her promise,
    Kept it at a fearful cost,
For she swore to shield Naomen
    Though her life thereby she lost.

" ' So I told her, and the traitor
    Stands before the council now,
Let the fate the tribe allots him
    Fall upon no other brow.

" ' I was honored by these people,
    And by them in illness cared,
And their food, and salt and hearth-fire
    I have with them often shared.

" ' I am old, and gray, and withered,
    But I fear not Death's worst pains,
For the blood of countless sachems
    Courses in Naomen's veins.'

" Scarcely had these words been spoken
    Ere his plume was cut in twain,
And a Mingo's heavy hatchet
    Cleft his skull-bone to the brain.

" Thus he died, and with him perished
    Both the settler and his wife,
For naught else availed the warriors
    Save the sacrifice of life.

" This my story," said the Indian,
  "And among you is there one
Who has heard of deed more noble
  Than this by Naomen done?"

All were silent, and no answer
  From the listening trappers came,
For they felt as if the savage
  Put their boasted deeds to shame.

TO THE LOVED ONES IN SANTA CRUZ.

THE GIFTS I ASK OF THE NEW YEAR, JANUARY 1ST, 1888.

THE merry bells are pouring out a pæan on the air,
   Away with 'Eighty-seven—a welcome to his heir,
A step is on the threshold, the New Year 's at the door,
He stands before me with his pack, the Old Year is no more.
A stranger to the century—I throw the portals wide,
A youth of gallant bearing is standing by my side.

A welcome to the stranger ! I trust a kindly fate
Will strew thy path with blessings, oh! year of 'Eighty-eight,
I know the brothers of thy line, their forms, their deeds, their
      dreams,
From 'Fifty-four to 'Eighty-eight each face familiar seems,
The thread of silver on my brow shows that I knew them
      then,
For halting step and silvered locks they ever give to men.

Oh ! years, that weave so much of care amid the woof of life,
That make our pathway here below a field of rugged strife,
I ask not for the golden boon the alchemists long sought,
I would not stay Time's furrowing hand upon my temples
      wrought.
I ask not these, but on the forms of those I love, I pray,
Let Time's relentless, iron hand upon them gently lay.

Where the Pacific's sunny slopes in golden splendor lie,
Where with the tinted Southern skies the blushing roses vie,
Where the wild ocean's foaming surf on cliffs of verdure beat
And falls in clouds of silvery spray upon yon headland's feet,
Where nestling,'mid her orange groves,an earthly Eden woos,
I see the vine-clad hills and vales of sunny Santa Cruz.

Upon that willowy figure there I ask your softest touch,
Bring back the roses on her cheek—this surely is not much,
Tint with the skies her tender eyes, bring back the azure hue,
That long ago, in other lands, an ardent lover knew,
And to those lips, whose coral tips a lover sighed to taste,
Give all those charms your elders gave to soft Diana chaste.

And last of all, I ask of you, ere comes the flowers again,
To strew with verdure and with light Missouri's fertile plain,
Guard well my sweetheart far away on the Pacific slope,
Keep light the heart that beats for me, bright tinge each
    thought and hope,
Speed well the train that thunders fast o'er gulch and moun-
    tain gray,
Give her safe back to arms that love—these are the gifts I
    pray.

WITH WASHINGTON ON THE DELAWARE.

DECEMBER 25 and 26, 1776.

'TWAS a cold night in December,
   The sky was bleak and bare,
The swiftly falling snow-flakes
   Were whirling through the air.

Within, a glowing wood-fire
   Blazed forth its ruddy light,
As if to hurl defiance
   At the cold and chilly night.

The room was warm and cosy,
   It was filled with Christmas cheer,
There were pies, and cakes and cider,
   And huge mugs of home-made beer.

The elders sat and chatted
   Of the doings of the week,
While the children in the corners
   Were playing hide and seek.

Where the fire-light was brightest,
   On a wide, well-cushioned chair,
Carved in quaint and curious fashion,
   An aged man was resting there.

THE VETERAN'S FIRESIDE.

Page 79.

He was a stout old soldier,
　Of the grim Provincial line,
Who had fought the French at Quebec,
　And his King at Brandywine.

His breast was seamed and sunken
　Where a bayonet, glancing, broke,
And a scar was on his forehead
　From a Hessian's sabre stroke.

The fire blazed and crackled,
　The children's games were done,
Their elders in their arm-chairs
　Were dozing one by one.

A cold draught from the entry
　Blew upon the old man's hair,
Lifting it from off his forehead
　Till the sabre gash shone bare.

The children round him gathered,
　They wished to hear him tell
Of the battle fields and marches
　Where he bore himself so well.

The old man looked upon them,
　As they nearer to him drew,
And upon their upturned faces
　An eager look there grew.

"And so you'd like old Father Green
    To tell of Eutaw's day,
Of Germantown and Monmouth
    With the Brunswickers at bay.

"My share in all those battles
    With the hirelings of the Crown,
You've heard me tell you often
    Of how we mowed them down.

"But I'll tell you now another,
    Whose scenes a bright look wear,
How with Washington's Provincials
    I crossed the Delaware.

"I was with the patriot army
    In that winter cold and gray,
Where, not thirty miles from Trenton,
    It in winter quarters lay.

"Every day our army dwindled,
    Every day it smaller grew,
Some were sick, and some had left us,
    And their number was not few.

"We were worn from cold and hunger,
    None were fit to face the storms,
And our clothes were but mere tatters,
    For we had no uniforms.

" Yet you should have heard the cheering
　That within our quarters rose,
When we heard there was a prospect
　Of a combat with our foes.

" We were soon drawn up in columns,
　And the march was then begun,
For we wished to be near Trenton
　Ere had dawned another sun.

" A wild snow-storm was raging,
　And the wind a fierce gale blew,
Cutting to our very marrow
　As our rags it whistled through.

" On we stumbled mid the snow-drifts,
　And before 'twas fairly night,
We had reached an open country,
　And the river was in sight.

" There it flowed, a sullen current,
　Blocked with cakes of floating ice,
And it seemed as if our frail boats
　Would be crushed as in a vice.

" The orders soon were given,
　The boats with men were lined,
Our oarsmen seized the paddles,
　And the shore was left behind.

" The storm beat in our faces,
   The ice ground 'gainst our boat,
We were so heavy loaded
   We could scarcely keep afloat.

" We looked not on the river,
   Our eyes were fixed away
Where Washington's tall figure
   Loomed upward dark and gray.

" Our weak boats groaned and quivered,
   Yet not a boat was lost,
We soon had reached the landing
   And the Delaware was crossed.

" The shivering, half-clad soldiers
   In line again were drawn,
And we were close to Trenton
   At the first gray streaks of dawn.

" We could hear the distant shouting
   Of the Hessians, mad with wine,
And the eyes of every soldier
   With a purpose fiercer shine.

" They were holding yet their revels
   Of the Christmas scarcely passed,
But they little thought or reckoned
   That to some 't would be the last.

" We had seized their sleeping picket,
  And upon our foe dashed down,
Just as Forrest's heavy cannon
  Opened on them in the town.

" 'Twas a scene of wild confusion,
  Half-dressed soldiers crowd the street,
While their officers are shouting,
  And the drums the roll-call beat.

" Fiercely, then, we press upon them
  And our volleys swiftly pour,
While Sullivan's field-pieces
  Answer Forrest's with a roar.

" Suddenly we see a horseman
  Spurring hotly to the front,
Well we know both horse and rider
  Come to bear the battle's brunt.

" The gold lace on his shoulder
  Marks an officer full well,
For it is the Hessian Colonel
  Of whose deeds we oft heard tell.

" He soon a squadron rallied,
  And with drawn sword at their head,
The crimson-handed troopers
  He in person on us led.

" Then came the clash of sabres,
And I saw my comrade reel,
He fell from out his saddle
Pierced by their leader's steel.

" He was a youth of nineteen,
A gray-haired widow's son,
His brothers fell with Warren,
And his sire at Lexington.

" My sabre had been broken,
My pistol missed its aim,
And with a shout of triumph,
Bold Rahl upon me came.

" An officer was falling,
I seized his dropping blade,
And, ere it could be parried,
A deadly thrust I made.

" His sword drops from his fingers,
He no longer guides his horse,
For the Grenadier of Brunswick
From his charger falls a corse.*

" The Hessians were disheartened,
Some were captured, others dead,
And with terror, panic stricken,
The few survivors fled.

---

*Col. Rahl, the Hessian commander lived six hours after the engagemen .

" We fired a few more volleys,
    Then the bloody work was done,
The white flag rose before us,
    And the hard-fought field was won.

" I turned my foaming charger,
    When the smoke-clouds cleared away,
I saw an officer approaching
    Upon a mettled bay.

" 'The General, sir, he wants you,'
    Said the aide-de-camp to me,
'You'll find him in that tent, sir,
    Where yon fluttering flag you see.'

" I put spurs to my charger,
    The distance soon I went,
The sentinel on duty
    Showed me within the tent.

" I halted by the General,
    At his side stood Knox and Stark,
He was engaged in writing,
    And my entrance failed to mark.

" His brow, which had been darkened,
    Brightened up as I drew near,
And turning from his table,
    He thus spoke loud and clear :

" 'Your brave deeds in this battle,
    Deserve my thanks full well,
But a Captaincy of Rifles
    My thanks can better tell.'

"I tried to thank the General,
    But all things seemed to whir,
My tongue and limbs grew rigid,
    I could neither speak nor stir.

"He beckoned to a soldier,
    For my thoughts he clearly read.
'Show the Captain of the Rifles
    To Lord Stirling's tent,' he said.

"I reported then to Stirling,
    But I scarce had left his tent,
When a sudden pang shot o'er me,
    And through vein and artery went.

"Ah! I knew what that keen pang meant,
    Ere gushed forth the red'ning tide,
It was from a musket bullet
    That had struck me in the side.

"I had felt it in the action,
    When we fought there blade to blade,
But I thought it merely grazed me,
    Or a scratch had simply made.

" Then a mist rose up before me,
    And I sank upon the ground,
And for days and weeks together,
    I was dead to all around.''

There was silence by the fire-light,
    And the old man's eyes were dim,
While the children, lost in wonder,
    Gazed in silent awe on him.

But he saw not their young faces,
    His thoughts were far away,
He was on the stormy Delaware,
    At the early dawn of day.

TO MY WIFE.

JANUARY IST, 1889.

A T thirty-five, all men agree, the poet's muse should own
   To wear a garb of more sedate and sober hue and
      tone;
'Tis said it ill becomes a man, with children eight years old,
To play the gallant troubadour and write in fashion bold.

The day of lyrics long has past, sonnets should turn to prose;
The man with temples turning gray should sing not of the
      rose.
These follies do for youthful days, when men are hot in
      speech,
But passion has no place in life when thirty-five you reach.

Thus speak the mentors of our day; but somehow, on my life,
My muse will play me curious tricks, when thinking of my
      wife,
And all the precepts moralists lay down as fitting age
Vanish, whene'er my fancy turns to Bessie's lovelier page.

And well they may, for loveliness is rare so fitly clad
Since woman's charms in Eden's day the heart of man made
      mad;

88

No wonder, then, the poet yields allegiance to thy spell
And bows in homage to the Queen, who wields Love's sceptre
well.

The hair may silver with Time's flight, the eyes grow weak
and dim,
And blood may not more swiftly flow at sight of ankle trim;
Not so the muse, if touched by love, whatever men may say,
The muse of twenty is the muse of thirty-five to-day.

I feel it so this glorious morn, as at your feet I fling
The brightest New Year wishes that the poet's verse can
bring;
May all the gifts the fairies weave for those they love be
thine,
Strew naught but roses on her path, oh! year of 'Eighty-Nine.

What of the thorns, the cruel thorns, that stem the roses
sweet?
I ask that these be swept aside, nor touch her tender feet.
Throw them upon the poet's path, for he has trod, men say,
From Chaucer's age to our own time, naught save a thorny
way.

A DREAM OF ETHEL AND JUNE.

THE sun of a summer morning
　　Sifts soft through the old oak trees,
And the boughs of the top-most branches
　　Are stirred by the summer breeze.

The song of a distant robin
　　Comes carelessly to my ear,
And the music of children's laughter,
　　When I listen, I can hear.

But the world around is forgotten,
　　To its visions dead I seem,
Could you glance at your lover's figure
　　You would almost think I dream;

Yet my thoughts have only wandered
　　To the dim and forgotten days,
That live in Life's purer annals
　　Touched with a hallowed haze.

A thousand glowing fancies,
　　Fancies dear to a lover's eye,
Such as born of a poet's longings,
　　Ever live in a lover's sky

Have sprung into life and being
   At the touch of Love's quickening tunes,
As I call back the golden memories
   Of the dead and forgotten Junes.

But brighter than these comes the picture
   Of a certain blonde-haired girl,
Who stands midst the other maidens,
   The Queen of them all—the pearl.

A form whose every motion
   Is as lithe as the willow trees,
When the leafy forest giants
   Are swayed by the bending breeze ;

Eyes in whose dreamy fire
   A tropical passion is hid,
Veiled from the light that they rival
   By an arched and quivering lid ;

Arms in whose snowy whiteness
   The dimples mirrored lie,
Like the clouds that float in the morning
   On the breast of a summer sky.

In her face a ripple of sunshine
   From the heaven above seems wrought,
And her cheeks a tinge of color
   From the tint of the rose have caught ;

A wealth of tender, true love
　Looks out from her heavenly face,
Pure as the bosom beating
　'Neath the tremulous folds of lace,

As she sits by the swaying rose-bush,
　And dreams in a girlish way
Of the plighted troth she has given
　And her lover far away.

And the heart of him she dreams of
　Keeps time to the magical glow,
That sweeps in a crimson torrent
　From her brow to her bosom of snow.

But ah ! what a fond foolish lover,
　Here, where June's sunlight soft gleams,
You smile at his visions and fancies,
　Born, you say, of a lover's warm dreams ;

Fit only, you say, for a dreamer,
　Fit only for June and its breeze,
But perhaps it were best for us all, love,
　To have more such thoughts as these ;

Such pure and tender fancies,
　That come but too rare in life,
To temper the heart for its struggle
　In this world of sin and strife.

At least so I think this morning,
  As under the oak tree's shade,
At the feet of a distant maiden,
  These day dreams of love are laid.

TO THE ST. JOSEPH HIGH SCHOOL ALUMNI.

AT THE RECEPTION TENDERED THE CLASS OF 1875, JUNE 18, 1875.
AS RECITED BY MISS LILLIAN M. TOOTLE.

I.

O MUSE of song! O Muse of light!
   Fling me your mantle but to-night;
Fain would I give my rugged lay
The gilding of thy brighter ray,
And throw o'er every word and line
The magic of thy art divine.

II.

'Twas given in the olden time,
When to the ocean's surging rhyme
The God-like bard responsive spoke,
And glory's echoing answer woke—
'Twas given then; pray, give me now
A chaplet from thy laurelled brow.

III.

On Memory's wings once more we glide
Over the Past's fast ebbing tide,
And fancy again around us plays
As gaily as in our youthful days,
When life seemed like the merry song
That the wafting breezes carry along.

94

IV.

The scenes that Youth so highly prize
Again appear to our dazzled eyes,
We drink again of the ruby cup,
With Pleasure's red wine bubbling up,
And as the generous wine is quaffed,
We forget the dregs that line the draught.

V.

But away with the vague and shadowy Past,
That round us its weird-like spell would cast,
We have long since left that sunny land,
And are far away from its golden strand,
And its shores are now but dimly seen
Through the billowy wastes that lie between.

VI.

We turn to the Class, whom to-morrow's day
Will usher into the world's great play.
Their hearts are to-night as free from fears
As ours were in the long ago years,
When on the banks of Life's swift stream,
We first saw its eddying waters gleam.

VII.

But the roseate pictures which once we drew,
Melt like the mirage from our view,
And the mingled dreams of fame and power
That together dawn on Life's opening hour,
Are rudely shattered and tossed aside
By the onward surge of Time's hurrying tide.

VIII.

For the future rarely proves as bright
As 'tis pictured by Fancy's glowing light;
And the fairest colors fade fast away
Under the withering heat of Time's pitiless ray,
And Youth's gayest, brightest, happiest page
Is dimmed by the quivering hand of Age.

IX.

But why do we speak of the clouds that rise
And dim the fairest of earthly skies,
For is not the rainbow of Hope always seen
Through the mists of distrust that intervene?
And does not the future always seem fair
To those whom Life's freshest garlands wear?

X.

And, perhaps it is better after all
That they see not the Future's dark'ning pall,
For may not a grander portal be won,
When the cares and strife of life are done,
By the steady faith and the hopes that are born
When we stand on Youth's brightly breaking morn.

TO ALICE.

A NEW YEAR GREETING.   JANUARY 1, 1890.

FLING up the portals of the years—a new decade is born !
  The 'Eighties are but shadows grim, the 'Nineties
    greet the morn.
I hear the ring of merry bells from out yon chapel's walls,
As on the frosty winter air their silver paean falls.

Hail to the new ! 'twas ever thus since the first century's
    dawn,
Le Roi est Mort, Vive le Roi, the phrase was aptly drawn,
Empires and thrones are fleeting toys in manhood's deeper
    game,
But human nature mid the strife is ever found the same.

Perhaps 'tis well, and yet a boon I crave, New Year, of you,
'Tis not for fame, or wealth or power, that I a suppliant sue,
These are but baubles ; I would fain a nobler guerdon pray,
Oh ! year of 'Ninety, do not smite, thy hand of iron stay.

Touch gently form and feature rare, dim not those radiant
    eyes,
In whose soft depths I ever see the azure of the skies,
Add not a thread of silver to those coils of golden hue,
Give not a pang to that fond heart, that beats so warm and
    true.

No longer chime the distant bells—I start in my arm-chair,
Before me bows a gallant youth—'tis 'Ninety standing there,
No need, said he, the boon to ask, I bend, too, at her shrine,
Such loveliness and graces rare are safe from darts of mine.

Well said, New Year! I wish that you could gaze upon her
    face,
You'd surely own my lips have failed to half portray her
    grace,
No need, said he, to paint her charms, no words can jus-
    tice do,
For I looked within her window pane before I bowed to you.

THE ROSE AND BESSIE'S PICTURE.

ON the stand with your picture one bright summer day
    A rose for a moment I chanced there to lay,
'Twas a rose of the forest, of the rarest known kind,
Such as bloomed in the Paradise Eve left behind,
So crimson its petals, so tinged with soft flushes,
I can only compare them to your sweetest of blushes,
And so lovely its bearing, so modest its air,
Methought it and the picture must form a twin pair;
But the rose had scarce given one glance at your face
Ere I saw that a rose-bud had taken its place,
Surprised at its action, I asked of the rose
What caused it thus quickly its petals to close?
It blushed, as it answered, what rose could presume
To nestle beside one of lovelier bloom?

99

THE POET'S VISION.

JANUARY 1st, 1891.

A GRAY sullen night and a cloud-flecked sky,
  The night's shadows grim on Time's dial lie;
Fit time to muse, as I silently gaze
On the flickering light of the hearthstone's blaze.

And the years roll back, again I stand
On the shadowy borders of "no man's land."
As I see, iris hued, the mirage of years
That only in dreams and to youth appears.

The scroll of the world with the very same guise
It has e'er borne to dreamers—like a buccaneer's prize,
The earth lies before me, its wealth and its fame,
The tribute man's genius should rightfully claim.

The ardor of youth again thrills my veins,
As the poet's fond vision my fancy enchains,
And in the sweet glance of Nellie's gray eyes
Is borne the soft radiance of Eden's lost skies.

The curtain of years from Life's drama rolls back,
The 'Seventies dawn upon youth's vista-hued track,
And "the light that is never on land or on sea"
Shines full in the face of sweet Nellie and me.

Paints her eyes with the skies, tints her face with a blush
Such as brought to her cheek the carmine's soft flush,
When, for weal or for woe, bringing rapture or strife,
She plighted her troth and her fealty for life.

The bride of October before me appears,
With the smile on her lips half denying the tears
That sprang to her eyes, as she soft speaks the words
That mate hearts for life as are mated the birds.

Steals a chill winter morn from its mantle of gray,
As the sunbeams of dawn from the night break away,
And on a low cot, like a benison rest,
Where a baby's head lies on a mother's fond breast.

But hark ! on the night air there falls a sharp stroke
And the dreamer of dreams from his vision awoke,
The clamor of bells tells the New Year is here
And chimes a soft dirge to the vanishing year.

All hail to the New Year so gayly begun,
I kiss my hand to thee, oh ! year 'Ninety-One,
On my sweetheart and child shed your softest of beams,
And do not forget the old dreamer of dreams.

ADELE.

I.

THERE are fair names, I own it, whose soft, liquid sound
  Make the pulses leap higher, the very blood bound,
The Maudes and the Carries, the gay laughing Lous,
The Lizzies, the Fannies, the wild, dazzling Prues;
They are charming, I know it, yet show me a spell
Such as clings to the name of my witching Adele.

II.

I have looked into eyes that were melting and true,
Eyes that rivaled the azure of heaven's own hue,
Eyes flecked with soft hazel, eyes beaming and bright,
In whose depths lay imprisoned the darkness of night;
Yet their glances were harmless, they wanted that spell,
That gleams in the glance of my charming Adele.

III.

You may speak of the maids of Circassia's white sands,
Of the passionate daughters of sunnier lands,
How on their soft cheeks, 'neath a tropical sun,
The rose and the lily are blended in one;
I grant you this freely, but I know, ah! too well
There are none that can equal my darling Adele.

IV.

But hark! on my musings there breaks a soft note,
'Tis the cadence that wells from a distant bell's throat,
As it pours on the air in a clear, liquid sheet,
The tones that now echo adown the long street;
But, were it my fate, a far sweeter bell
Should ring to the name of this same fair Adele.

TO———

BRIGHTER than the brightest gleams,
   Erring mortals see in dreams,
Shimmering o'er with fitful glow
Seething brain that throbs below,
Is the maid to whom alone
Every womanly charm is known.
Mingled thoughts of her tonight
O'er my fancy cast their light,
Drifting scenes of fairest hue
O'er my rapt, enchanted view,
Now the present fades away
'Neath the past's entrancing ray,
Every scene in color glows,
Life again its passion knows,
Love again in fancy glows.

THE RHYME OF THE WEDDING RING.

A VISION OF NEW YEAR'S EVE.

I.

WHERE rolls a mighty river through gulch and gleam-
              ing bar,
Where mountains raise their summits and snows eternal are,
Where torrents dash through canyons and rugged pine trees
       stand,
I see the scheming Spaniard's dream—the El Dorado land,
The land that Ponce De Leon sought, that proud Balboa saw,
As on the lofty mountain peak he stood in fear and awe.

The actors shift before my eyes, the centuries roll between,
Fades Spanish knight and buccaneer, I see another scene ;
In place of steel clad men at arms appears a fairer sight,
As on the pine clad mountain slopes are ranged the tents of
       white
Where live the men of '49, who sought as did of old
The Argonauts of Jason's day, the glittering fleece of gold ;

I hear the woodland echoes ring, I see the pick-axe bright,
And list to tales that miners tell around the fires at night,
Bold, swarthy men of iron mould who hold their very lives
Clutched in their brawny, sinewy hands, as hunters hold their
       knives,

And see the golden nuggets gleam in buckskin belt and pouch,
And hear the sullen panthers' cry that in yon thickets crouch.

II.

Fades mining camp and mountain slope—a city's crowded
    street,
Where traffic toys with idleness, my wandering eye doth
    greet,
There heaps of shining metal lie, I see the furnace glow,
And at my feet a molten thread begins to softly flow,
And what the cunning alchemists in vain assayed of old
Is wrought within a moment in yon seething mass of gold.

I hear the whir of moving wheels, the engines puff and roar,
And plunged within a sulphur bath are bars of virgin ore
To rise again, with dripping sides, a glittering mass of gold,
Enough to buy a monarch's crown in the dim days of old,
More than enough, in later days, to bring heads to the block,
To raise vast armies into life, and thrones and empires rock.

Then comes a group of artisans who hammers deftly swing,
And soon the yellow bar of gold becomes the shapely ring,
A circlet fit to grace the hand of peasant maiden fair,
Or brightly shine amid the gems that deck a princess rare,
When knightly gallant stoops to woo and courtly maid to
    hear,
When blushing cheek the story tells, as well as glistening
    tear.

III.

I see a crisp September night, a fire-side's softened glow,
A taper on the mantle that sheds its rays below,
A maiden, coy and winning, with a rose bud in her face,
Whose luster mocks the blossom that doth her corsage grace,
A form of heavenly symmetry, cast in earth's loveliest mould,
Such as artists limned in ages past and minstrels sang of old ;

I see the blush grow deeper still upon her heavenly face,
I note her breasts' soft heave and swell beneath their folds of
  lace,
Again I hear the flattering tale that love and passion pour
Into the ear of listening maid, as they have done before,
Since Helen heard her praises sung, since Abelard's far day,
Has taught the ages yet to come Earth's one immortal lay ;

I hear the lover's ardent words, his fond and burning tones,
As to the maiden of his choice he love and fealty owns,
I see the glittering circlet pressed on yielding finger tip,
Ere yet the kiss of plighted troth has touched the upturned
  lip,
And read the eager, whispered words, the fervent, tender
  sigh,
Which bears to lips that bend above Love's answering reply.

IV.

But hark ! on my visions and fancies there breaks a solemn
  note,
'Tis the New Year's happy paean, flung from a church bell's
  throat,

It vibrates through soul and being, as I list to the echoing
    strain
That brings to my wearied spirit its long lost youth again,
And I sit and vaguely wonder, as the poet's song I sing,
Whether eyes that I love will moisten at the rhyme of the
    wedding ring.

AT THIRTY-EIGHT.

JANUARY 1, 1892.

I HEAR from yonder swaying tower the ringing chime of
    bells,
The cadence from their brazen throats a New Year's birth
    foretells,
The clock has struck the midnight hour, the Old Year's course
    has run,
The night winds sigh thy requiem, oh, year of 'Ninety-One !

The spectral shadows of dim years their phantoms round me
    cast,
Strange figures of forgotten days, ere Youth's bright dreams
    were past ;
The 'Seventies have come again, I see their blithesome forms,
And live again their radiant hours, nor fear Life's threaten-
    ing storms.

I see a cosy cottage brown, set 'neath a church's spire,
Within whose sheltering parlor walls there glows an old time
    fire,
A maiden fit to grace a throne, a trim form set in lace,
The roses in her bosom pure rest in a fitting place ;

Swift fly the hours when youth and maid together converse
    hold,
When at Love's first confessional the one sweet tale is told
That marked the dawn of Eden's day, that blushed in Eve's
    fair face,
The one sweet strain of Paradise which Time cannot erase.

The 'Eighties pass before my eyes—a mother's tender face
Bends o'er a cradle in whose depths her counterpart I trace,
The love that lived for me alone now knows a sweeter tone,
Such as comes only to the breast which motherhood has
    known.

The 'Nineties dark before me rise, the whitening touch of
    age
Has set his seal on hand and brow and closed Youth's sunny
    page,
I feel life's heart-beats fainter grow, I mark the shadows
    gray
That sweep o'er Life's meridian with sunset's closing ray.

My eyes would pierce the veil of night, I start in guilty fear,
Why dim the New Year's welcome with trace of coming tear,
Nay, rather hail him gladly, a youth of gallant form,
With mien of royal bearing—an oak to face the storm.

A beaker to the New Year! I fain would ask thy grace
To touch not with your graver a line of Bessie's face,
Cut deeply in my forehead the lines that best suit you,
But leave my darling scatheless, oh, year of 'Ninety-Two!

A NEW YEAR RETROSPECTION.

THE clock upon the mantle piece has struck the midnight
    hour,
The chime of bells rings gaily forth from yonder steepled
    tower,
The air is vibrant from their throats, alone I sit and muse,
Why is it with Time's frosting touch the hopes of youth we
    lose ?

Do hearts grow old with passing years? Alas! it must be so,
The heart of youth would ill become a head so touched with
    snow,
Who plays Life's game with Father Time plays e'er with
    loaded dice,
For youth and its impassioned joys come ne'er to mortals
    twice.

Perhaps 'tis better as it is that to man's longing eyes
Comes only on this earth of ours one glimpse of Paradise ;
It were not well with mortals here were Earth's stern barriers
    riven,
And to the world worn mariner too much of Heaven were
    given ;

Yet I will ask a boon today, oh, year of 'Ninety-Three !
Out of the favors in thy store, grant one, I pray, to me,
Within the heart of him who pleads ambition long has fled,
And all the ardent dreams of Youth are withered, cold and
    dead.

He feels the frosts of ripening years, his powers begin to
    wane,
And ne'er will hand, or tongue, or brain their cunning find
    again,
His spirit, broken, longs for rest, he views the setting sun,
With him, at least, he knows full well the best of life is done.

He asks you, then, oh ! coming year, ere yet thy dawn's full
    flush
Has tinted hill and landscape with its golden, radiant blush,
To guard the loving ones at home, and shield them from
    Life's storms,
And let the ruder blasts of Earth ne'er touch their tender
    forms.

On Mother, Wife and Baby dear, thy richest gifts bestow,
The're worthy of the precious boon, oh ! year, I fully know.
If you must give the bitter draught, and pathways rough be
    trod,
Let him who asks thee for thy gifts bow to the chastening
    rod.

IN INDEPENDENCE HALL.

A DREAM OF THE REVOLUTION.

THE summer's sun is falling
   About me as I stand,
And gaze on the faded portraits
   Of the founders of our land;

On the grand and noble faces
   That hang from the paneled wall,
On the rich and heavy mouldings
   Where the gathering shadows fall;

And my thoughts go backward drifting
   To the dim and misty days,
That live in a Nation's legends
   Tinged with a golden haze;

When the tread of stout John Adams
   Re-echoed through the halls,
And the fiery words of Otis
   Rang out upon these walls;

When the Continental Congress
   Struck freedom's first key-note,
And the Bell of Independence
   Flung it from its brazen throat.

They were no common heroes,
  These men of iron mold,
Who founded the Republic
  In the stormy days of old.

And when the shades of evening
  In the hall begin to creep,
A score of spectral faces
  Before my vision sweep.

At the head of the phantom figures
  That tread the old oak floor,
Comes the stately form of Hancock
  In the courtly garb of yore.

A quick and ringing footstep
  Bursts on my listening ear,
I could touch the cloak on his shoulder
  As he hurries by me here.

'Twas General Lee that passed me
  In his youthful vigor and pride,
I forgot the field of Monmouth,
  And his scornful words beside ;

Then Jefferson advances,
  A leader among men,
Who severed a tyrant's shackles
  By a stroke of his glowing pen.

He is standing now by Franklin,
 As he stood on that July day,
When the destinies of a Nation
 In the wavering balance sway;

At his side a slender figure,
 'Tis the form of Hamilton,
Wearing well the garnered laurels
 He in field and forum won.

On his brow no brooding shadows
 Of that morning, chill and gray,
When beside the Hudson's waters
 Slowly ebbed his life away.

There is bluff old Baron Steuben,
 And the gallant Lafayette,
Whose dark blue regimentals
 Full well his figure set.

How the heart of every patriot
 Thrills at that noble name,
Rich in its deeds of glory,
 And its heritage of fame!

A spurred and booted trooper
 Steps from an archway tall—
Mad Anthony's lithe figure
 Swings lightly down the hall;

I see the Maumee's waters,
    And the bivouac at night,
The savage Shawnee faces,
    And Paoli's red'ning light.

Thus they pass in review before me,
    These men who the king defied ;
But a group of gallant soldiers
    Have halted at my side,

Hale and Knox and Mercer,
    And bold Nathaniel Greene,
And amidst the other faces,
    Pulaski's, too, is seen,

I see him hurl his troopers
    On the crimson British line,
When he led the charge in person
    On the field of Brandywine.

They stand—the scarlet troopers,
    Drawn up in grim platoons,
But they break in wild confusion
    Before his fierce dragoons.

He had fought in other battles,
    On a far-off, foreign shore,
Ere had set the Star of Poland
    On a red'ning field of gore.

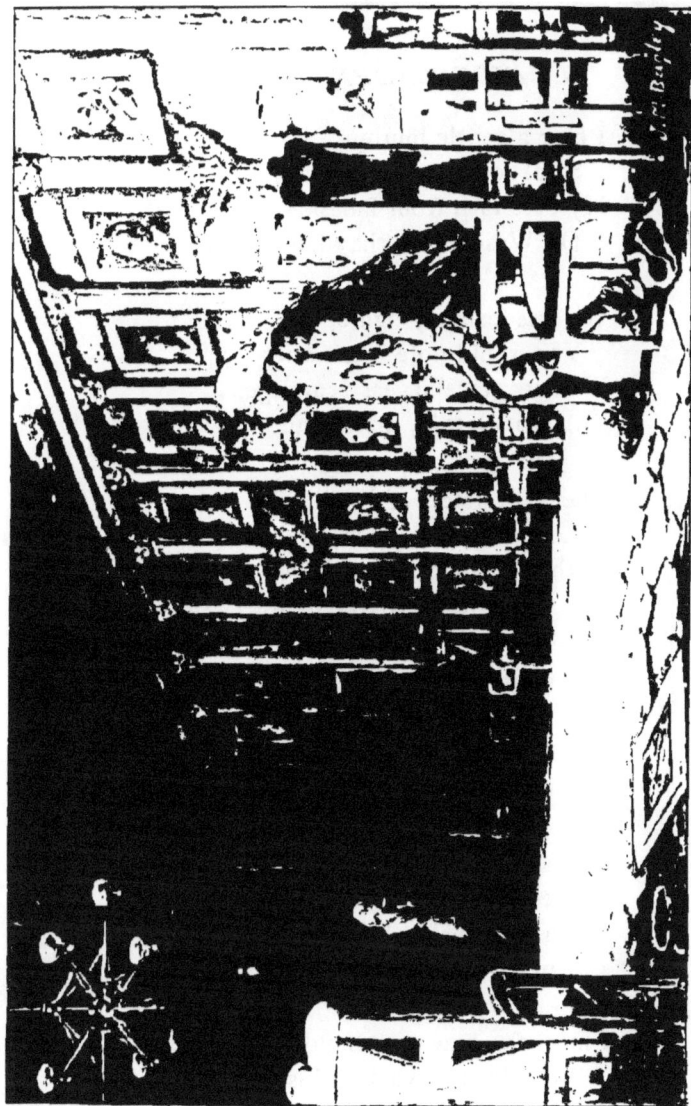

THE SPECTRAL FIGURE IN THE RECESS.

Page 119.

I hear a gentle murmur
　Steal softly down the hall,
My eyes turn from Pulaski—
　On Washington they fall.

His was a stately figure,
　You would note it anywhere,
With its graceful, easy carriage,
　And its lordly, martial air.

The wild defeat of Braddock's
　Looms upward on my sight,
With the gallant young Virginian
　In the thickest of the fight.

The scenes of the revolution,
　They pass before me now,
Till I see him stand at Yorktown
　With a calm, unruffled brow.

But hark! from a shadowy recess,
　I seem to hear a groan,
I peer into the darkness—
　A man stands there alone.

I meet the gaze of Arnold
　As he looked when in his prime,
Ere his strong arm had been palsied
　By the weight of a traitor's crime.

He looks on the moving pageant
  With a wan and haggard face,
And on his haughty features
  A tear drop I can trace.

I start from my midnight dreamings
  Of the men of olden times,
As I hear the silvery pealing
  Of a distant church-bell's chimes.

I wake—to find the faces
  Have vanished from the hall,
And the pictures still in their places
  On the dusty, paneled wall.

SWEET NELLIE STEVISON.

A TOAST.

YOU may talk of circlets flashing at some dainty maiden's
   throat,
As the glitter of rare jewels mid her bosom's lace you note,
How the eyes that bend above them, to a youthful gallant's
   sight,
Mock the flash of gem and jewels by their radiant, tender
   light ;
I will grant the yielding homage youth to beauty ever pays,
But I bow before no sceptre save the one my Nellie sways.

You may speak of regal beauty, of the fair, voluptuous
   charms
That the waltz's wooing measures have enfolded in your arms,
How the queenly gaze that meets yours, as it pierces to your
   heart,
Wakes the dormant fire and passion that to life and being
   start ;
Well I know the force of passion, of its fierce, impulsive
   storm,
But to me it bears the image of my lovely Nellie's form.

You may tell of eyes of azure, cheeks that mock the blushing
   rose,
Such that in the glowing summer to a June day's sun unclose,

Form as stately as the lily, lips whose curves of luscious red
To the crimson of the cherry and the carmine's hues seem
    wed ;
Charms like these, I grant you freely, but in Nellie's face are
    blent,   ·
All the mingled charms that sunshine has to rose and lily
    lent.

And when the clash of clinking glass meets that of brimming
    cup,
From out yon glittering flagon's depths I fill my goblet up,
When gallants speak of beauty's glance and fill the beaker
    high,
And as they tell of women fair, the generous draught drain
    dry ;
I speak of her whose charms I sing, of her whose heart I've
    won,
And give the evening's fittest toast—sweet Nellie Stevison.

ON PARTING WITH EVA.

A SEEMING PARADOX.

THERE'S an adage or legend, believed by us all,
    That man below angels but little doth fall,
Of all legends or stories, to this one alone
No single exception had ever been known,
Till one evening, my darling, in parting with you,
Your dear little self to my own side I drew,
And as your cheeks crimsoned with Love's vivid flame,
Your soft silken tresses to my shoulder but came;
And I found that the adage could never be so
With the sweetest of angels a full head below.

123

A NEW YEAR GREETING.

JANUARY 1, 1894.

TIME'S clock has struck the Forties—the year's life's knell
    has spoke,
Tolled from its brazen, iron tongue at every vibrant stroke;
Passed now is Life's meridian, the bloom of manhood's
    prime,
The flowers that line the pathway of Youth's enchanting
    time;
From now nought but the sunset—the shadows lengthening
    grow,
Age creeps upon Time's dial, Life's pulses sluggish flow.

In vain the sage has written: 'twas ever thus with man,
The Fates have e'er decreed his years should be a narrow span
Between the fleeting centuries—why strive to pierce the veil?
Remember that the mariner who fain his barque would sail
O'er unknown seas and trackless wastes must make his faith a
    chart,
And steer o'er hidden shoal and sunken ledge with the
    Genoan's gallant heart.

No need the pulses slower beat, the hair its sprinkling gray,
The eye its dimming lustre to tell of fell decay,
The heart has felt its icy touch, the spirit once of oak,
Beneath Earth's bitter struggles at last has bent and broke,

Ambition's joys that flamed so bright to ashes long have
    turned,
He humbly pleads but now for rest who once all rest had
    spurned.

'Tis bitter thus to see the dreams we cherished in youth's
    prime
Vanish and fade, as all things fade with manhood's dull de-
    cline,
And Earth's horizon smaller grow upon our dimming eyes,
And know its sky no longer holds a dream of Paradise;
The heart will murmur at its lot, will turn with vague unrest,
And question in its bitterness the solace of the blest.

I turn from Life's harsh questionings—my heart's blood
    swifter flows,
For in sweet Bessie's upturned face the rose of youth still
    glows,
Those soft red lips have not forgot the witchery that they
    knew,
When once they murmured long ago that they would e'er be
    true.
What if Life's clouds do lower dark, a Heaven's yet on earth,
And one fond glance of those soft eyes can give it life and
    birth.

But hark ! a chime of silvery bells from out yon steeple high,
Rings out a merry greeting to the somber wintry sky ;

A truce to Forty and its cares—oh, year of '94!
Strew on the path of those I love from out your well-filled
  store,
The choicest blessings in your pack, and if you've any over,
I fain would in my meadow plant a little of your clover.

THE GOOD SHIP 'NINETY-SIX.

WHAT OF ITS VOYAGE?

I.

ABOVE a dark December sky, the night is waning fast,
The Old Year from its moorings slips—a spectral
figure vast,
Without, a gallant vessel rides, trim every spar and sail,
A hull of oak to breast each sea and ride each threatening
gale,
Ruddy her glow from christening blow, for wine and brine
ne'er mix,
The staunch craft in the offing there—the good ship 'Ninety-
Six.

II.

And as the white sails catch the breeze that ripples o'er Life's
sea,
I wonder if the pleasant sight a harbinger will be
Of goodly voyage, free from wreck and storm, of quiet port,
Such as the world-worn mariners who sail the seas e'er court,
Of sunny isles, 'neath southern skies, where stately palm
trees grow,
Of tropic waters fathoms deep, whose depths with coral glow.

127

III.

But shadows gather on the sky, I see another sight,
A good ship labors in the sea—afar the wrecker's light,
I hear the distant breaker's roar, the drifting surf's white
    foam
A requiem plays to bark and crew that o'er mad billows roam,
When lightning flashes show a face, a mast, and then a spar,
And morning breaks upon a sea, whose waves no wreckage
    mar.

IV.

What picture holds the future? I strain my dimming eyes,
Alas! the seer's keen insight beyond my vision lies;
Will yon stout ship, at anchor ride, within the coral isles,
Where fronded palm to rippling wave 'neath tropic splendor
    smiles?
Or will a shapeless wreck float by and on the shoals be cast,
Little to mark the once proud bark save broken spar and
    mast?

V.

Oh, good ship in the harbor there! I pray thee voyage fair,
To every soul on thy staunch deck, a fellow-seaman's prayer,
God speed you on your outward course, set well your helm
    and sail,
Fear not the wrecker or the shoal, nor yet the driving gale;
I ask of Him who rules the seas, who bids its tempests cease,
Bring yon brave ship and all its crew safe to the port of
    Peace.

www.ingramcontent.com/pod-product-compliance
Lightning Source LLC
Chambersburg PA
CBHW030617270326
41927CB00007B/1209